MW00900483

Being Human

A chapbook of selected essays
A love letter

Ellen,

Thank you so much for all of the encouragement and support! Enjoy.

Sean

Being Human

A chapbook of selected essays
A love letter

John Sean Doyle

Rainstick Press
2015

Copyright © 2015 by John A. Doyle, Jr.

All rights reserved. This book or any portion thereof may not be reproduced or used in any manner whatsoever without the express written permission of the publisher except for the use of brief quotations in a book review or scholarly journal.

First Printing: 2015

ISBN 978-1-329-48051-3

Rainstick Press
4006 Barrett Drive #104
Raleigh, NC 27609
Raleigh, North Carolina 27608
www.JohnSeanDoyle.com

Ordering Information:

For all inquiries, please contact the author at J.SeanDoyle@gmail.com. Special discounts are available on quantity purchases by corporations, associations, educators, and others.

For Jenny,
Andrieu, Abigail and Allison.

"I said to the almond tree, 'Sister, speak to me of God.' And the
almond tree blossomed."

— Nikos Kazantzakis, Report to Greco

Contents

John Sean Doyle

Frequented by Longing: An Introduction

To live entails a certain amount of longing. Sometimes the feeling lays dormant within us, year-after-year, just beneath the surface, as if we were only lingering until death. We pass time at the mall or some job or doing the dishes. We wait in some line that resembles some other line we'd stood in a thousand times before, going nowhere. And then one day something changes. Maybe we were passed over for a promotion we never wanted. Maybe the doctor gave us a diagnosis. It could be, we had to watch helplessly as someone we love - a child, a spouse, a sibling, a friend - suffers some great pain or grief or loss. Or maybe one day, someone we trusted, someone we depended upon for so much, unexpectedly smashed everything we'd ever believed in and ordered our lives around.

Or the change might not have been prompted by anything in particular. We simply woke up one day, literally and figuratively, and pushed aside the covers to recognize in a very real and very personal way, the shortcomings and impermanences and limits of being human and alive.

How are we to live such a world? We leaf through the pages of the sacred texts. We wring beautiful truths from antiquity's scrolls. We plot what science has taught on distribution curves. However, sometimes what we want and need and long for is simple validation of where we are in the struggle. To be given hope and reasons to hope. To be assured that while the things of life can be hard, difficult, scary, irrational, unjust and unfair, that fundamentally there is no reason to fear or fret or fade. There is always, always just-cause to love life and to celebrate the tender, rapturous, beautiful intimacies that also are our inheritance. We are not the first ones in this world to suffer or struggle or doubt. We won't be the last. And there is comfort in knowing we never need go it alone.

I want you to believe in fairy tales again. I want you to believe in the goodness of people, that there is beauty all around us, that there is reason for hope, and that you are better than you thought you were. Science and experience have shown these things to be true. Each one of us has at our finger tips access to so much meaning and hope, goodness and beauty in every moment, if we would only let ourselves see.

My hope is that this sampling of essays, selections from a longer collection, will comfort without pretense, assure without pretending to know the "answer." Informed by the science but suckled on poetry, occasionally these exercises in humanity just might stumble across something that resembles what it means to live the world, beautifully and passionately, with honesty, integrity and grace.

A full book is on the way. Please register at my site so I know where to find you: http://www.johnseandoyle.com/register/

Sean Doyle

September 17, 2015
Raleigh, North Carolina

John Sean Doyle

Clinging to Truth, Clinging to Kindness

Sometimes things in life happen that shatter your world. Not just the expected traumas, as raw and difficult as they may be: The death of a loved one, or how, with the passage of time, we watch our own decay. Even if we have banished these inevitable facts of our lives to the farthest edges of possibility, somewhere beneath awareness we know that one day they will occur. As hard and as real as they are, they were written into the script before we began. Human beings are evolved for adaptation. With time, clinging to what centers us, and a little holding of hands, we will endure, and even thrive.

But what happens when the hardship, the trauma, cuts directly at that which centers us? When the unthinkable strikes those beliefs that were our foundations? What about when the things we relied upon in structuring and ordering our lives can no longer be trusted? How are we to respond when we lived our lives as if the world were good and safe and beautiful, and someone or something ripped that from us along with our hearts?

Of course, I am not six years old. I know bad things happen and that sometimes people take advantage of the innocent, vulnerable or trusting. Injustice has been with us longer than Christ. I am not talking about a loss of innocence that, to a certain degree, is part of normal maturation. Rather, what happens when another being betrays our trust in such an intimate way that there is nothing left of what we believed about the world?

Giving up, or giving in to despair, is easy and natural. But it can never protect or heal. In the face of hardship, injustice or the coldest of traumas, the only answer is love. When everything is out of control, the only thing we can do is give ourselves over to a universe we cannot control and hold even tighter to kindness. Even if the pain we feel was caused by people-upon-people, the only response that can save us, is caring even more deeply.

Being Human

As soon as we stop caring and stop being surprised at the world's unjust indiscretions, we lose that which is the most human thing about us. Anger burns everyone. Especially the one who holds it. Yet to take refuge in love, we are healed again, purified, and the ground is prepared for new growth.

I know it sounds naïve or trite to say that in the face of hardship or trauma, the only answer is love. However whether in the workplace, our personal lives, or even the tight spots in life, both research and experience prove this to be true.

As a five or six year old child, I used to go with my parents to visit an elderly relative. Alcohol, anger, and hardship had ravaged her for years. I don't tell this story to shame or blame in any way. We don't get to choose the angels or demons that take up residence in our lives. We wrestle with the torments as best as we can, but sometimes we are overwhelmed.

My parents would send me to the playground or to the next room to watch reruns in black-and-white as they helped her with her taxes, her medical issues, and other troubles. Over the static of the TV, I remember her screaming at them, and my father gently handing her groceries or money to help with her bills. I don't know what was said. I don't know what my parents wrestled with privately or together back at home. But I did see that under duress, they fed her kindness. All those years ago I was too young and tender to notice, but those moments of respect and care and calm were my first lessons in subtlety.

Conflict is inevitable. The weak will be exploited. You will be hurt by your friends and loved ones. Coworkers and strangers will insult and belittle you. People can be remarkably cruel. But none of this means that violence in inevitable; not physical violence, not emotional violence, not verbal violence, and not even an anger held in our hearts. There is one response that is both effective and allows us to maintain our sense of integrity, humanity and respect: love.

You are cut off in traffic. A coworker sends you a snippy email. Your teenager rolls her eyes at you. You are passed over for a promotion. The homeowner's association sends you a certified letter complaining that you left your garbage at the curb too long. At the church fish fry, a neighbor spreads gossip about a friend. When the other responds to us with a poke in the eye, it is easy to feel hurt, frustrated, and angry.

Sometimes we try to persuade them with reason. Sometimes, we want to hit back. When a cyber-bully lobs condescending or incendiary bombs at us in public, it feels good to beat them over the head with their own stupidity or triteness. A violent repartee to violence feels justified. In our counter attack, we feel vindicated.

But hours later, back at home again, reliving the experience with friend or spouse, our heart is still racing and our blood pressure, still climbing. So often, any trace of a positive feeling that accompanied the sense of justification falls away, and we feel a little dirtier, and a little cheaper, that we allowed ourselves to be made worth less.

Further, it is unlikely that the hostile response even worked. After disabusing the bully, does he have a moment of clarity and insight, apologize, and thank you for showing him the error of his ways? Of course not. Maybe he tucked his tail between his legs and briefly stopped his public ranting, at least for now. However, the only thing violence really does is dehumanize the other. While it may have appeared to work in the short term, it does not really *work*.

Violence always hurts someone, somewhere. We know it hurts the recipient. But tragically it also hurts us, and it injures any witnesses to the carnage. How we treat one another spreads outward through networks and effects strangers and loved ones alike.

Cacioppo, Christakis, and Fowler have shown that happiness, loneliness, altruism, and whether people cheat all spread through networks. If people cooperate, it is more likely that strangers, three degrees removed, will also cooperate. Like an event cone, one act, whether it inserts humanity or hostility, changes and alters seemingly unrelated events.

It is this dynamic that lay behind what Gandhi called *satyagraha* or soul force. The strength of non-violence is not in weapons or numeric advantage, but in clinging to truth. It is not easy or soft or passive. It does not involve ignoring injustice or wishing it would go away. Rather satyagraha's steadfast commitment to humanity and refusal to inflict harm can take tremendous strength, courage, and stamina. It requires you to stare unblinkingly in the face of hostility for extended periods of time, under extreme conditions, with no guarantee that you will be successful in the immediate situation.

Very often, increasing humanity in the midst of crisis might not feel like it works. Cheaters often get away with it. People who stab us in the back or suck up at work, sometimes get rewarded. However often it does work in the short term. As a lawyer who has negotiated over 10,000 disputes, I have seen this again and again. An invitation to understanding, empathy, or respect, gives the other a backdoor out of their own hostility and a pathway to resolution.

Importantly, as peace scholar Michael Nagler points out, while nonviolence sometimes works in the immediate moment, it always *works* on a larger scale. If we interrupt the violence and insert humanity into inhuman situations, that goodness, kindness, and love will also spread and affect how others deal with one another. We might not be immediately aware of how or why. However when we increase the humility, compassion, understanding, vulnerability, kindness or love, somewhere it will heal and build.

For psychiatrist George Vaillant, we were meant to be bound together. Our brains are wired for social connection: for love, respect, appreciation, acceptance, sympathy, empathy, compassion, and tenderness. These are the things that connect us. These biologically-based, spiritual emotions reach the other at levels that pure reason can never touch. Satyagraha does not change the positions of the parties. It changes their relationship.

When my parents responded to a drunk, despondent and aggravated old woman with compassion and respect, they did not know that this kindness would reach the child quietly listening in the next room, plant seeds in his soul, and continue to grow outward for forty years.

Whether we are seeking peace in middle school or the Middle East, whether the bully is in the lunch room or the board room, in most circumstances, the most effective strategy is the one that increases the amount of humanity between people.

References & Further Readings

Cacioppo, J. T., Fowler, J. H., & Christakis, N. A. (2009). *Alone in the crowd: The structure and spread of loneliness in a large social network.* Journal of Personality and Social Psychology, 97(6), 977-991

Christakis, N. A. & Fowler, J. H. (2009). *Connected: The Surprising Power of Our Social Networks and How They Shape Our Lives.* New York: Little, Brown.

Heschel, A.J., (1999, 1955) *God In Search of Man*, New York: Farrar, Straus and Giroux.

Nagler, M., (2001). *Is There No Other Way? The Search for a Nonviolent Future.* Berkley Hill Books: Berkley.

Vaillant, G. (2008). *Spiritual Evolution: A Scientific Defense of Faith.* New York: Broadway Press.

John Sean Doyle

Hugging the Horse's Head

In January 1889, Friedrich Nietzsche went insane.

Armed with metaphor, irony and aphorism, the German philosopher carved his influence deep into 20th century culture, criticism, literature and psychology. Freud, Mann, Yeats, Richard Strauss and countless other artists and thinkers were shaped by the "first Immoralist". In popular culture, Nietzsche was idolized and vilified for his Zarathustra coming down out of his cave in the mountains with an eagle and a staff and declaring that god was dead.

But despite the death of god, despite the nihilism and the altered manuscripts, Nietzsche's writing affirmed life. It was filled with courage. Nietzsche embraced the hardships, boundaries and sickness of the world and called upon each of us to stretch beyond the social constructs of culture and the moral legacy that is our inheritance.

But then on January 3, 1889, everything unraveled. While in an open air market in Turin, Nietzsche witnessed a merchant flogging a horse. He ran to the animal and yelled for the beating to stop. He threw himself between beast and whip, and hugged the equine's thick neck. This frail and sickly philosopher who gave us the Übermensch and slave morality, then collapsed, weeping.

I understand why Nietzsche hugged the horse's head. Life is hard. It is not fair. It is filled with rapturous beautiful moments and it all ends much, much too quickly. When we look around and see so many people who are unnecessarily cruel, or mindless, or oblivious to inequities; when we see our brothers and neighbors exhaling their numbered breaths in ways that add to the pain or take from the sympathy, we see a world that is, in fact, more absurd and nihilistic than anything the philosopher wrote or said or thought. To see these mindless cruelties playout before him was simply too much for the philosopher to bear; especially when the remedy, the antidote - even our purpose for being here - is so very clear.

Nietzsche was a pastor's son. Raised on nagging hypocrisies and half-truths of a faith half-applied, Nietzsche rejected everything. The prophets did too: Jeremiah and Isaiah, Mohammad and Siddhartha. Even Christ. But whether obvious or ironic, the remedy was there, at the center, all along. It is that certain truth, absolute but malleable, at the center of every faith tradition. We look up from our desks or push ourselves away from the table and see people treated unfairly at work or on the playground or at the church fish fry. It happens in our very own homes. Yet all any of us need, all every one of us need, is understanding, patience, kindness, and simple human respect. Every one of us is just bumping around trying the best we can. Everyone one of us is dealing with the same raw adaptive imperatives: births, deaths and the sufferings and sicknesses of loved ones. We wake in the morning with a new tumor or must move our bowels in a bag hung under our shirts or we struggle to find answers or reasons for so many human dilemmas that are simply a part of living. No wonder sometimes we ourselves can be unknowingly cruel or thoughtless or rudely blunt. Yet we are all just doing our best. In a world where we all make mistakes, where our motives are misunderstood, the only answer that makes sense is to give ourselves over to kindness, forgiveness, patience and understanding.

Go down to the marketplace. Empty your pockets of fear and self-consciousness. Lay everything you are out bare on a blanket. Exchange what you thought was in your "best interest" for a more humane humility. For one day, the horse's head we will be hugging, will be pointing toward eternity.

John Sean Doyle

References & Further Readings

Thus Spoke Zarathustra. trans. Walter Kaufmann, in *The Portable Nietzsche*. New York: Viking Press, 1968.

Wicks, Robert, "Friedrich Nietzsche", *The Stanford Encyclopedia of Philosophy* (Winter 2014 Edition), Edward N. Zalta (ed.), URL = http://plato.stanford.edu/archives/win2014/entries/nietzsche/

See also, *Because I Could Not Stop for Death*, from *The Poems of Emily Dickinson*, Ralph W. Franklin ed., Cambridge, Mass.: The Belknap Press of Harvard University Press, Copyright © 1998 by the President and Fellows of Harvard College.

Whatever Happened to Conner MacBride?

Thoughts of peer pressure bring a parent's worst fears to mind: sex; drugs; uncategorized acts of stupidity; the fact that our kids cannot be who they are, when they are, the most themselves. When they get home at night, there is no escape from the peacocking of peers on Instagram and Vine, teasing over twitter, or the torment on Facebook. And even we, in our adult dignity, are not immune. There are the ladies in the garden club with their hats; the bosses whose only ethic is a personal P&L; and gossip at the church fish fry. How many times have we watched as someone was treated unfairly at work, and yet we could not intervene?

There is another kind of peer pressure too.

One night sometime back in high school when we were still young and indestructible, we were out drinking too much with friends and the friends-of-friends. These were not the "good" kids. They were the ones who smoked between class, if they went to class at all. They got into fights and got suspended. They painted curses on the walls. Several of the boys had used the heaviest drugs, the ones we were taught to fear. Yes, I drank, and I was too young. But I never was tempted by or desired those other drugs.

But on this night of whisky, beer and diminished judgment, someone pulled out psychedelic mushrooms and it caused me to pause. They seemed more interesting. They seemed more aligned with my seventeen year old poetic and philosophic nature. So as the plastic bag was passed from person-to-person sitting in a circle on the floor, my curiosity and interest grew.

To my right sat Conner MacBride. We were friendly, no doubt, but he was not among my closest friends. He consumed the heaviest drugs in the largest portions. There were rumors about is home.

Rumors that no one wanted to imagine true. Sometime much later, he would be kicked out of school and sent away.

The mushrooms were passed from hand-to-hand, from stranger-to-friend and to Conner MacBride. Then, suddenly, they leapt past me in a toss. Conner MacBride, that lotus-eater, the child that all of the parents feared, looked me straight in the eyes, raised the whisky bottle level with our gaze, and told me with great sobriety that if he ever heard I was doing drugs, he would smash the bottle over my head. "You are the only one in this room that has a chance," he said, "you are worth more than this."

Where did you go, Conner MacBride? What happened to you, and to all the people in our lives, those somewhere between friend and stranger, who watch over us from the margins and shadows like angels who have fallen and know how much it hurts?

Our friends will be there for us time-and-time again, year-after-year, but sometimes they too will let us down. Sometimes our dearest friends are the ones who administer the pressure we fear. They are after all, just as flawed and tempted and confused as any of us. Honor this truth. Forgive them. Keep them in your hearts. But sometimes what we need are our tarnished peers. Sometimes the pressure from those around us is not something to be feared. Tender moments are often shared in the harshest of ways and in the darkest of places.

I don't know now if I would have tasted the mushrooms on that night. Or if I had, whether the arc of my life would have shifted. But looking in the dilated unblinking eyes of someone no one trusted, I learned that trust was the only thing that mattered. That the day-in, day-out decency we offer one another, that our humanity demands we offer, sometimes makes a difference without us ever knowing. That if we honor ourselves by honoring others, that others will be there in dark rooms giving back, so brutally, so beautifully.

Further Readings

Buber, M., *I and Thou*, (W. Kaufman, Trans) New York, NY: Charles Scribner's Sons (1971, first published 1923)

Kapuscinski, R., *The Other*, Verso (2008)

Keltner, D., *Born to Be Good: The Science of a Meaningful Life*, W. W. Norton & Company (October 2009)

Ricard, M., *Altruism: The Power of Compassion to Change Yourself and the World*, Little, Brown and Company; Tra edition (June 2, 2015).

John Sean Doyle

Learning to Ride a Bicycle

In those long summer days when the children were young and desperate to ride a bicycle, I would take them to a field behind the school, or out to the park, where the grass would be forgiving of tender elbows and chins. Their excitement was tactile, honest. With rapt attention, my daughter kicked one leg up over the seat. Self-confident, but with enough nervousness to make her alert, attentive. How could I expect her to know any risks beyond rumors of skinned knees; Risks that I, grown wise and timid, saw behind every dandelion and buttercup? Holding her and her bike firmly, I began to run. Slowly at first, with a steadying hand, but increasing in momentum as she peddled faster and faster.

This scene has of course, passed. All my children are grown now. My joints no longer allow me to chase behind bicycles. And while the memory perches in my mind like a nightingale on a green branch, it too will fade as silently as a bird passing on its way to the horizon.

Yet these are the moments that make me believe that permanence is possible. Ceremonies of innocence happen unscripted every day. In every country, every era, *Innocence* unclasps her hands and lets our children loose into the uncertainty.

I never wanted to let go. I never did let go. Exuberant and determined, my daughter peddled harder and harder and pulled away from me. She wobbled and swerved into the future with confidence and grace. There is nothing about a parent's fear that can ever change that.

Permanence is not this one moment on a bicycle. The facts of the different time and different place vary and prove unimportant. Maybe it was that boy sailing ships in the *Jardin du Luxembourg*, using his wooden stick to navigate "salty oblivion". Or maybe that girl in a long dress, tossing and catching the inflated bladder of a pig, forever preserved in oil by some Dutch master. Our children touch the things of death so lightly and yet their smiles require no translation. The dangers I fear are real. They exist in the vacant lots where boys in dust-rag shirts swing cricket bats as if there were no other joy. And they are there on the city streets filled with strangers: the same streets and same strangers given music by the child pressing bottle caps to the bottoms of his sneakers to make tap shoes and beg for coins. And the worst torments of all are the internal fears and doubts, the self-criticisms invisible to my protective gaze. When little girls who believe in pig tails run, please let it always be to kick a crushed soda can overflowing with laughter and dreams. That afternoon in the park with my daughter was one of the immortal moments given me, timeless, fleeting, but that provides luminance between two everlasting darknesses.

How many more times would I have to watch or imagine as she goes forward in a world that doesn't always have soft fields to break her fall? When she pulled away balanced on a bicycle, she did not look back over her shoulder. But letting go does not have to mean having to go it alone.

The whole of my life has been about learning this balance. In my teens and early twenties I felt an existential howl deep in my bones. No one could ever know me. No one could ever feel what I felt. The face I showed to the world was only what was safe and expected, but could never reveal those deep things inside me that no one could ever accept. I was as anxious to be free as a child on a bicycle, but chained in my own aloneness.

As I got older, I discovered I was not alone. I discovered that love was not about me, or whether some "she" returned my gaze. Rather love was about caring, caring about another more than I cared for myself. The joys of a child on a bicycle completed me and filled whatever holes I thought were in my character and in my soul.

But now my temples grey, I did not expect this new, deeper aloneness. Alone and helpless, having to watch the ones you love navigate the hardness of the world. For the universe is thick with harsh things that no child, no one, should ever have to face or confront or endure.

With unbounding innocence, my daughter imagines herself ready for what lay beyond the horizon. And yet I know it is too big. I am an optimist and will forever believe in the inherent goodness of people, yet I know the world is too unforgiving. At some point in our lives, between seventy and ninety percent of us will experience a severe traumatic event. Forty-three percent of kids have already done so before they turned 18. Someone is sexually assaulted in the US every 2 minutes. Teen depression and psychopathology has risen five-fold since the early part of the 20th century.

In India, there is a belief that when a child is born some god or goddess comes down and writes the details of its life on its forehead. Every joy. Every spider bite. If I could only see. Which of the facts of her destiny would I try to erase? Which sufferings would build her up, and which pleasures bring her down? As if somehow, I could guarantee for her a world that was fair and just and always kind.

But I cannot see, and a new aloneness creeps in.

There is nothing about life or trauma or suffering that scares me. I have learned that I am strong enough to withstand any hardship. But what of the hardships that do not befall me? What of those traumas that slip from the fingertips of the cosmos as unevenly as ash spread by a dove at sunset, and land on my children or spouse or dearest friends?

What can we do? The world is the world regardless of what I think or hope or pray. If I can no longer stand behind my children steadying them what can I do?

Let them know that you love them. Let them know that whatever secrets they hold, whatever impure thoughts they have had or deeds they've done, that nothing can dull their luster.

Let them know that they are more than one thought, or one moment or one mistake. Let them know that whatever bad things happened, nothing can bind their present or corrupt their future. Their lives and happiness are not dictated by events or the past.

Teach them that bad things will happen to them in life. The world is filled with many things, and many of those things are terrible. It is not fair. We might not understand why. But teach them to always, always look for what good they can take from whatever life hands them. Because there will always be something that can help nurture and strengthen them. Maybe they will discover that they are stronger than they thought they were; better able to cope; better able to hold others afloat. "What could life ever do to me now after I have lived through this?" Maybe when bad things happen they will notice the unexpected people who rush to their aid and comfort. It will not always be those they expected, but there will always be helpers. We are not alone after all. It is just that the angels in our lives might not be known to us in this moment. Maybe in the face of something horrible, they will find the grace and strength and insight to rewrite the story of their lives to be one of coherence and clarity and even kindness. Maybe they will realize that many of the things that they thought were so important, really do not matter anyway. Maybe they will see that no matter what, they have the power to infuse kindness and hope and meaning into the lives of others.

Help them – your children, your spouse, those you love - to see that they are more humanly perfect than they believe. Let them know that they complete you.

Permanence is not some unbroken chain in my consciousness or memory or understanding. It cannot be plotted out on some line graph. All of us participate in a serial permanence – the same struggles, the same traumas, the same joys – that have always been with us. And all of us have the power to find meaning and relief and happiness in our lives, by creating meaning and relief and happiness in the lives of those around us. Loving strongly does make us vulnerable. But so to, it is the love that counteracts the grief, heals us, enables forgiveness and awe, gives us purpose and joy, and makes us complete.

References & Further Readings

Borchard, T. (2010, March 4). *Why Are So Many Teens Depressed?* Retrieved September 17, 2015, from http://psychcentral.com/blog/archives/2010/03/04/why-are-so-many-teens-depressed/

Eckes, A. and Radunovich, H. L. (October 2007. Revised August 2015). *Trauma and Adolescents* (Publication #FCS2280). Gainesville: University of Florida Institute of Food and Agricultural Sciences. Retrieved Sept, 2015, from http://edis.ifas.ufl.edu/fy1004

Kent, E. (2009). What's Written on the Forehead Will Never Fail: Karma, Fate, and Headwriting in Indian Folktales. In *Asian Ethnology* (1st ed., Vol. 68, pp. 1-26).

Tedeschi, R. G., & Calhoun, L. G. (1996). The Posttraumatic Growth Inventory Measuring the positive legacy of trauma. *Journal of Traumatic Stress*, 9(3), 455-471.

Tedeschi, R. G., & Calhoun, L. G. (2004). Posttraumatic growth: Conceptual foundations and empirical evidence. *Psychological Inquiry*, 15(1), 1-18.

Twenge JM, Gentile B, DeWall CN, Ma D, Lacefield K, Schurtz DR., Birth cohort increases in psychopathology among young Americans, 1938-2007: A cross-temporal meta-analysis of the MMPI. *Clin Psychol Rev*. 2010 Mar;30(2):145-54. doi: 10.1016/j.cpr.2009.10.005. Epub 2009 Nov 5. Retrieved from http://www.ncbi.nlm.nih.gov/pubmed/19945203

Vaillant, G. (2008). *Spiritual Evolution: A Scientific Defense of Faith*. New York: Broadway Press.

Zagajewski, A "Try to Praise the Mutilated World" from *Without End: New and Selected Poems*. (Farrar, Straus & Giroux, LLC, 2002)

For a few examples of children playing with pig's bladders in art See Pieter Bruegel the Elder's *Children's Games* (1560); Isaac van Ostade's *Cut Pig* (1645); Isaac van Ostade's *Stabbed Pig* (1642); and Egbert van der Poel's *Barn Interior* (1646).

Encounter: An Invitation

The short selection of essays in this chapbook is just the start of what I hope will become an active and ongoing dialog.

First, it is a dialog between you and me. Register at my site below and leave comments on the articles. Share the essays and your thoughts with your family and friends and neighbors. Take an active part in the discussion, because ultimately, the words on these pages are about your life. A full book is on the way and I need to know where to find you.

Second, I hope that the essays here and on my website contribute, even if only in some small sense, to the swath you want to carve in the world. Put down your phone. Let screen on your computer or tablet gently nod off to sleep. Go with your friends and loved ones to a park or a coffee shop or some other quiet spot and look them in the eyes. Discover once again their hopes, their wishes for the future and their fears. It is our dreams that make us different than the mud beneath our feet.

And just as every other finite and infinite point in the universe, you are changing and growing. The people dearest to you are changing and growing. They are different now from who they were when you first fell in love. In so many subtle and not so subtle ways, they are even different than who they were yesterday.

With fingers interlaced, trace with them the contours of everything beautiful and miraculous about your life and about their lives.

Being Human

Renew your love-vows and promises of the heart. Reminisce about the good things. Lend them a soft heart and strong back and help them shoulder their heaviest burdens. Help them to hold on or let go. Help them to hope again. Encourage them to chase their dreams with all the passion and care and tenderness of heart of someone desperately in love with life.

Your life matters more than you know. Cherish it. Celebrate it. Be good for the world.

Sean

www.JohnSeanDoyle.com

About the Author

A practicing lawyer for over twenty years, **John "Sean" Doyle** has negotiated more than 10,000 disputes and represented or advised hundreds of clients, including legislators and abandoned children, business leaders and the homeless, army generals and people fleeing torture. While working closely with people in the midst of conflict, or as they search for meaning in an often indifferent world, Sean continually finds the hope, goodness and beauty that is there.

A coach and frequent speaker, Sean has addressed these topics with individuals and groups as diverse as global law firms, army drill sergeants, federal judges, middle school children, Buddhist monks, and foreign governments.

Sean writes the *Luminous Things* blog for Psychology Today (www.psychologytoday.com/blog/luminous-things) and teaches positive psychology at North Carolina State University. He has also been a visiting scholar or guest lecturer at numerous schools including the University of Pennsylvania, Duke School of Law, Duke Divinity School and the University of North Carolina School of Law.

Sean studied philosophy at Rutgers, received his Juris Doctorate from Loyola University New Orleans, and his Masters of Applied Positive Psychology from the University of Pennsylvania. A husband and father of three, Sean lives and writes in North Carolina.

For information about Sean or to get news about the full book register at: http://www.johnseandoyle.com/register/.

You can also follow him on Twitter: @JohnSeanDoyle; and on Facebook www.facebook.com/JohnSeanDoyle

I stop somewhere waiting for you

- Walt Whitman